SOCIAL
MEDIA
SENSATIONS

Facebook

Joanne Mattern

Checkerboard
Library

An Imprint of Abdo Publishing
abdopublishing.com

abdopublishing.com

Published by Abdo Publishing, a division of ABDO, PO Box 398166, Minneapolis, Minnesota 55439. Copyright © 2017 by Abdo Consulting Group, Inc. International copyrights reserved in all countries. No part of this book may be reproduced in any form without written permission from the publisher. Checkerboard Library™ is a trademark and logo of Abdo Publishing.

Printed in the United States of America, North Mankato, Minnesota
062016
092016

THIS BOOK CONTAINS
RECYCLED MATERIALS

Design: Emily Love, Mighty Media, Inc.
Production: Mighty Media, Inc.
Editor: Liz Salzmann
Cover Photos: iStockphoto, Shutterstock
Interior Photos: AP Images, pp. 13, 17, 21, 23; Getty Images, p. 9; iStockphoto, p. 15; Niall Kennedy, p. 11; Shutterstock, pp. 4, 5, 7, 19, 24, 27, 29

Publishers Cataloging-in-Publication Data
Names: Mattern, Joanne, author.
Title: Facebook / by Joanne Mattern.
Description: Minneapolis, MN : Abdo Publishing, [2017] | Series: Social media sensations | Includes index.
Identifiers: LCCN 2016934272 | ISBN 9781680781885 (lib. bdg.) | ISBN 9781680775730 (ebook)
Subjects: LCSH: Facebook (Firm)--Juvenile literature. | Facebook (Electronic resource)--Juvenile literature. | Online social networks--Juvenile literature. | Internet industry--Juvenile literature.
Classification: DDC 338.4--dc23
LC record available at /http://lccn.loc.gov/2016934272

Contents

Facebook

URL: http://www.facebook.com

PURPOSE: Facebook is an **online** social-**networking** service. Users can communicate with each other, share photos and videos, and comment on what they are doing, thinking, or feeling.

CURRENT CEO: Mark Zuckerberg

NUMBER OF USERS: More than 1.55 billion

FEBRUARY 4, 2004
Facebook is founded

SEPTEMBER 2006
Anyone who is at least 13 can join Facebook

FEBRUARY 2009
The Like button is added to Facebook

MAY 18, 2012
Facebook becomes a publicly traded company

Meet the Founder

MARK ZUCKERBERG was born on May 14, 1984, in White Plains, New York. He attended Harvard University in Massachusetts, where Facebook began. When Zuckerberg entered Harvard, he already knew how to write several computer languages. He had also created several computer games. After creating Facebook, Zuckerberg left Harvard to run the site full time. He became one of the most important and influential business leaders of his generation.

Mark Zuckerberg

CHAPTER 1

What Is Facebook?

You're at a concert to see your favorite band. The lights dim and the first notes hit the air. You can hardly contain your excitement! You want to share these feelings. So, you post about them on Facebook. In seconds, your Facebook friends are sharing your experience.

Facebook is the most popular social media site in the world. It allows users to communicate with all their friends at once, and in many ways. Users share how they feel and what they are doing with written posts. They also share photos, videos, articles, and more. The possibilities are endless!

Facebook has greatly influenced the way people communicate. People use the site to connect with friends and make plans. They also use Facebook to send event

Facebook has a feature that notifies logged-in users about events their friends are attending.

invitations, record their experiences, and share important life events. Facebook has become a standard way for people to stay in touch.

CHAPTER 2

Facemash

Facebook began at Harvard University in Massachusetts. Nineteen-year-old Mark Zuckerberg was a student there. During his second year, he started a website called Facemash. Facemash was an **online** game using images of Harvard students. It allowed users to compare photos of students side by side. Users rated which was more attractive.

Zuckerberg got the photos by **hacking** into Harvard's online student **directories**, called Facebooks. Almost immediately, Facemash ran into problems. The students had not agreed to have their images used on Facemash. Many students were upset about being in the game.

Zuckerberg soon closed Facemash. However, many people had visited the site. This showed Zuckerberg that people liked to interact online through pictures. He began to think of a different way to let people share photos and information.

Zuckerberg (right) at Harvard with a classmate. He almost got kicked out of the school for creating Facemash.

CHAPTER 3

TheFacebook

On February 4, 2004, Zuckerberg launched a new website called TheFacebook. Anyone with a Harvard e-mail address could create a profile on TheFacebook. Users **uploaded** photos to their profiles. Then they added their interests, relationship **statuses**, and more.

Each profile on TheFacebook also included a page called a wall. Each person's wall could be seen by users the person had connected with, called friends. Friends could visit each other's walls and post messages to each other. Friends could also see and comment on what their other friends posted.

TheFacebook created an **online** community for Harvard students. The site was immediately popular. Within a few days, hundreds of students joined.

Zuckerberg speaking in 2011, in front of an image of his original TheFacebook profile

CHAPTER 4

Trouble and Growth

TheFacebook was very successful. But not everyone was happy with Zuckerberg's site. Three other students said Zuckerberg stole their idea. They were Divya Narenda and twin brothers Tyler and Cameron Winklevoss.

Harvard investigated the claims made by Narenda and the Winklevosses. The three students even filed a **lawsuit** against Zuckerberg. Years later, the lawsuit ended when Zuckerberg made an agreement. He gave the three men a cash payment and stock in the company.

In spite of its legal issues, TheFacebook continued to grow. At first, only Harvard students could join the site. But the **network** quickly expanded to other US colleges.

In 2005, Zuckerberg changed the network's name to Facebook. In September of that year, he launched a Facebook site for US high school students. It allowed the students to connect with each other.

Tyler (left) *and Cameron* (right) *Winklevoss and Divya Narenda* (center) *launched ConnectU, a site similar to TheFacebook, in May 2004. ConnectU shut down in 2008.*

By December 2005, Facebook had 5.5 million users. In February 2006, the company combined the college and high school sites. Now high school and college students could connect with one another.

CHAPTER 5

Big Changes

Zuckerberg knew he needed to keep his site adaptable. He would have to change Facebook based on **technology** improvements and his users' needs. So, in September 2006, there were two huge changes to Facebook.

The first was a change to the site's design. This included the new News Feed feature. Before this, users only saw friends' information by visiting their walls, now called Timelines. With the News Feed, logged-in users were brought to a constantly **updating** list of all their friends' posts.

At first, many users were upset by News Feed. Users were not prepared for their posts to become instantly visible to all their connections. However, users could change their privacy settings to avoid this.

Privacy settings allow users to make their accounts private or public. Content on public accounts can be seen by any visitor, even one without an account. Private accounts can only be seen by friends. Users can also organize their friends into groups and choose which groups see which posts.

The other big change affected Facebook's user base. Users no longer had to be associated with a college or high school. Now, anyone age 13 or older who had an e-mail address could create an account.

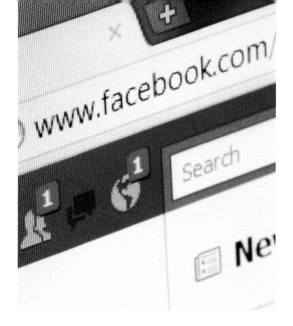

News Feed

Facebook's News Feed is a list of stories personalized for each user. To create a personalized feed for a user, Facebook **software** tracks what types of posts a user likes, comments on, and shares. Facebook also tracks how often a user interacts with each friend. Then Facebook uses the information to determine what types of posts the user is most likely to be interested in.

CHAPTER 6

Liking and Following

Facebook's popularity continued to rise around the world. In 2007, the site allowed businesses to join. Now, companies could create Facebook pages to share information and attract new customers.

In February 2009, Facebook introduced the Like button. Instead of becoming friends with a business, users could now like its Facebook page. The user would still see posts from the business. But the business would not see the user's personal posts.

Users could also like other types of Facebook pages. These include music groups, films, television shows, and public figures. And friends could like one another's posts.

Did You Know?

In 2011, the average Facebook user had 130 friends. By 2014, the average was 338 friends.

Many companies encourage consumers to connect with their brand, product, or service by liking their pages.

Facebook added the **Subscribe** feature in 2011. In 2012, the feature was renamed Follow. Follow allows a user to choose what type of each friend's posts will appear in the user's News Feed.

CHAPTER 7

Sharing and Linking

The average Facebook user has hundreds of friends. These connections can reach across the world! So, when a user posts content, many other users near and far can see it. And any content a Facebook user sees can be shared with his or her friends. In this way, posts, articles, photos, and videos can go **viral**.

Linking is another way Facebook posts can be spread. Facebook users can link their Facebook accounts with other social media accounts, such as Twitter and Instagram. Then posts on one account also appear on the linked accounts.

Facebook also links to other websites. Many businesses allow users to

Did You Know?

According to Facebook, the average user could read 1,500 posts each day, but views only about 300.

Facebook users shared more than 2.4 million pieces of content with friends every minute in 2014.

post content from the business's website directly to their Facebook accounts. This sharing and linking also makes it easy for content to go **viral**.

CHAPTER 8

Making Money

As Facebook continued to grow its user base, the company became very valuable. Many people invested a lot of money in Facebook during its first few years. This money allowed Zuckerberg to hire workers, rent office space, and grow his business into a worldwide **network**.

Facebook used investors' money to get started. But the site soon started earning money. Facebook's millions of users make it a powerful advertising tool. Ads can create interest in a product or service and direct traffic to the advertiser's website. Today, Facebook makes billions of dollars from companies paying to advertise on the site.

In 2012, Zuckerberg decided to make Facebook a public company. He did this by selling stock in the company on the stock market. Each buyer would own a small piece of the company. Facebook became a publicly traded company on May 18, 2012.

Crowds gathered in Times Square in New York City to witness Facebook going public.

CHAPTER 9

Social Power

Facebook has become a powerful advertising tool. It is also a powerful social force. People use Facebook to find out about and share developing news. This lightning-fast process helps information spread much more quickly than it ever could before.

Facebook is also used in social awareness campaigns. In 2014, a campaign to raise awareness of the disease amyotrophic lateral sclerosis (ALS) went **viral** on Facebook. The campaign was the Ice Bucket Challenge.

For the Ice Bucket Challenge, people dumped ice water over their heads. These acts were video recorded. Then people posted their videos on Facebook and named three friends to also take the challenge.

Everyone who took the challenge was also encouraged to give money to the ALS Foundation. Thousands of people took part in the challenge. In just a few months, more than $100 million was raised for ALS research.

Videos related to the 2014 ALS Ice Bucket Challenge were viewed more than 10 billion times on Facebook!

CHAPTER 10

Facebook's Impact

In addition to supporting social issues, many people form **online** communities through Facebook. These include fan clubs, book groups, job boards, and more. Facebook

Facebook is great way to connect with people online. But many people think social media makes users less social in real life.

groups help users plan events, interact with friends, and join new communities.

Facebook is a wonderful way to connect with friends, family members, and people with similar interests. It can inspire people to improve their lives. However, studies have found that social media, such as Facebook, can also have **negative** effects.

For example, people tend to only post positive information. This can create images of lives that are perfect and worry-free. Those false images can make others feel that their lives are not as wonderful as those of their friends.

Cyberbullying is another problem. Facebookers sometimes receive mean, hurtful comments or messages.

Did You Know?

Facebook users can choose from more than 70 languages!

Users should remember that real people are behind Facebook profiles! It's important to be kind when posting and commenting.

CHAPTER 11

Looking Forward

Facebook has changed a lot since its early days. What began as a **network** of college students is now a worldwide force used by more than one billion people. However, some think that Facebook is becoming less popular, especially among young people.

According to one study, Facebook lost more than three million teenage users between 2011 and 2014. The study found that young people are more likely to use other social media sites. These include Instagram, Twitter, Vine, and Snapchat.

In spite of this trend, Facebook remains popular. The company is always working to connect people in new ways. In 2015, Facebook announced plans to create a **virtual reality** experience. How Facebook continues to change as **technology** advances is yet to be seen. But its users are sure to play an important part!

Facebook remains wildly popular. As of December 2015, Facebook had more than 1 billion daily active users!

Facebook

A Facebook user must be at least 13 to have an account.

Once signed up, the user creates a profile. This includes **uploading** a photo as a profile picture.

Users can immediately start posting, uploading photos, and connecting with friends. Search for a friend's name in the Facebook search bar. To connect with them, send him or her a friend request.

Safety is important on Facebook. Users should not accept friend requests from strangers. Users should also not share personal information that could be used to find them in real life.

It's fun to comment on others' posts or photos. But Facebook users should remember to be kind. They shouldn't say mean things or bully anyone.

If a user receives rude comments, he or she should **delete** the comments. A user can block a bully from posting on the user's page. It's also possible to report **inappropriate** content to Facebook.

Glossary

cyberbully – to tease, hurt, or threaten someone online.

delete – to remove or eliminate.

directory – an alphabetical list of names or addresses.

hack – to get into a computer illegally.

inappropriate – not suitable, fitting, or proper.

lawsuit – a case held before a court.

negative – bad or hurtful.

network – to join or communicate with a group of people. The group is also called a network.

online – connected to the Internet.

software – the written programs used to operate a computer.

status – the condition of a person, situation, project, or event.

subscribe – to sign up to receive something on a regular basis.

technology – the science of how something works.

update – to provide new or current information about something.

upload – to transfer data from a computer to a larger network.

viral – quickly or widely spread, usually by electronic communication.

virtual reality – surroundings created by a computer that a person can affect and interact with.

Websites

To learn more about Social Media Sensations, visit **booklinks.abdopublishing.com**. These links are routinely monitored and updated to provide the most current information available.

Index